Sleepover Safari

written by Lucinda Cotter

illustrated by Lesley Danson

Engage Literacy is published in 2013 by Raintree.
Raintree is an imprint of Capstone Global Library Limited, a company incorporated in Engand and Wales having its registered office at 7 Pilgrim Street, London, EC4V 6LB – Registered company number: 6695582
www.raintreepublishers.co.uk

Originally published in Australia by Hinkler Education, a division of Hinkler Books Pty Ltd.
Text copyright © Lucinda Cotter 2012
Illustration copyright © Hinkler Books Pty Ltd 2012

Written by Lucinda Cotter
Lead authors Jay Dale and Anne Giulieri
Cover illustration and illustrations by Lesley Danson
Edited by Gwenda Smyth
UK edition edited by Dan Nunn, Catherine Veitch and Sian Smith
Designed by Susannah Low, Butterflyrocket Design

All rights reserved. No part of this publication may be reproduced, stored in a retrieval system, or transmitted in any way or by any means, electronic, mechanical, photocopying, recording or otherwise, without the prior written permission of Capstone Global Library Limited.

Sleepover Safari
ISBN: 978 1 406 26512 5
10 9 8 7 6

Printed and bound in China by Leo Paper Products Ltd

Contents

Chapter 1	On Safari	4
Chapter 2	Hippo Hooray!	8
Chapter 3	Making Camp	12
Chapter 4	A Visitor	16
Chapter 5	Brave Ria	20

Chapter 1
On Safari

"What if a wild animal tries to eat us?" said Ria, looking out of the truck at the safari park. Ria and her family had arrived for a special safari sleepover. But first, a guide was taking them to see the animals of the African savannah.

"Don't be such a scaredy-cat, Ria," snorted her brother, Marco. "These animals get plenty to eat. They wouldn't bother with a little kid like you."

But Ria wasn't so sure. The truck stopped suddenly, near a pride of lions. A large male with a big, scruffy mane, stood up and walked slowly towards them.

"Dad, save me!" cried Ria, covering her eyes.

Dad put his arm around her. "It's okay, Ria. You're safe in the truck. Look, over there! It's a giraffe!"

The truck started up again as a voice came over the loudspeaker: "The giraffe is the tallest of all mammals, with a neck almost two metres long." It was Fiona, their safari guide. "Did you know that giraffes only sleep for about two hours a day?"

Ria peeped through her fingers and watched as the giraffe stuck out its long tongue to pull some leaves into its mouth.

Chapter 2
Hippo Hooray!

Next stop was the hippo pond. Ria could only see the eyes, ears and nostrils of four hippos. Most of their bodies were under the water.

"The eyes, ears and nostrils of the hippopotamus are on top of its head," said Fiona, "so they can see, hear and breathe while they are in the water."

Just then, there was a loud snort and a jet of water sprayed the air. Ria jumped with fright as a hippo came up out of the pond. It opened its mouth in a wide yawn and showed its long bottom teeth.

"Ria's afraid of the hippos, too," Marco laughed. "Don't worry — they only eat grass, not little girls like you!"

The truck rumbled along past a family of meerkats. Some of the group were digging in the dusty ground while others stood on their back legs, keeping watch.

"Aren't they beautiful!" said Ria.

"And smart, too," added Mum. "They work as a team to look after each other."

"In half a day, a meerkat can dig 400 holes," said Fiona. "The black patches you can see around their eyes help protect them against the sun. It's a bit like us wearing sunglasses."

"I'd like to have one as a pet," said Ria, as she snapped a photo with her camera.

"Aren't you afraid it might scratch you?" Marco made his fingers into claws and growled at Ria.

"Cut it out, Marco!" she cried.

"That's enough," said Dad. "Look! You're missing out on the rhino." Sure enough, they were passing a huge rhinoceros.

"Look at that horn!" said Marco. "I bet that could hurt you. Watch out, Ria!"

Ria pretended she didn't care, but inside she really was afraid of the rhino's horn, and the hippo's teeth, and the lion's claws. How would she ever sleep tonight with wild animals prowling outside the tent?

Chapter 3
Making Camp

After the safari, it was time to go to the camp. Their home for the night was going to be a big tent with a wooden floor and mesh windows.

Dinner was an African barbecue feast. Then they sang songs and told stories around the campfire. Dad sang a song called "The Lion Sleeps Tonight". Then Marco changed it and sang "The Lion Eats Tonight", but Ria didn't think it was funny at all. In the distance she could hear the lions roaring. She shivered and cuddled up closer to Mum.

"Do lions sleep at night?" asked Ria.

"Oh, yes," replied Fiona. "They'll soon quieten down and go to sleep. And I think it's time for all of us to go to sleep, too."

As they made their way to their tent, Ria heard a snapping sound behind them. It sounded like twigs breaking. Perhaps one of the lions had escaped.

"What was that noise?" she whispered, hanging on to Dad's arm.

Suddenly, there was an enormous roar and something grabbed Ria's shoulders. She screamed. She was being attacked by a wild animal! But the wild animal stopped roaring and began laughing. "I got you that time, Ria," said Marco.

"Not funny, Marco," replied Ria, running the rest of the way to their tent.

Chapter 4
A Visitor

Ria felt warm and cosy in her sleeping bag, between Mum and Dad. It was quite dark, but she could see the moon and stars through the window of the tent, and she had her torch, just in case.

"The animals are behind a big fence, in their own special enclosure," Mum explained. "We're quite safe here."

Still, Ria could hear lots of strange noises in the dark — roars, snores, hoots and screeches. It took her a long time to fall asleep.

"Eeeeeeek!!!"

Ria woke suddenly. Something was making a terrible noise! And … the screech was coming from INSIDE the tent!

Ria grabbed her torch and switched on the light. The yellow glow shone around the tent. Mum and Dad were sitting up, too. Ria moved the light across to Marco. There he sat, as white as a ghost, with his mouth wide open. The terrible noise was coming from him!

"What's going on? What's the matter?" Mum sounded worried.

"There's something in the tent!" screeched Marco.

Chapter 5
Brave Ria

Ria shone her torch around the tent, but she couldn't see anything.

"This isn't funny," yawned Dad. "Stop trying to scare your sister and go back to sleep."

"I'm not joking," said Marco. He pulled his sleeping bag up under his chin. "I DID hear something."

Just then, they ALL heard a scratching sound, followed by loud scrabbling.

"Listen!" whispered Marco. "Did you hear that? There IS something in here!"

Now Mum and Dad looked scared, too.

Ria got out of her sleeping bag and shone her torch in the direction of the noises. Two beady eyes shone in the torchlight. Ria saw something small and brown, with a long thin tail. She tiptoed across the tent towards the small creature. A hungry rat was nibbling on an apple core that Marco had left on the floor.

"Get that rat out of here!" cried Marco.

Ria took a step towards the rat. It stopped nibbling and scurried away along the wall of the tent. Mum, Dad and Marco all screamed. Ria calmly lifted up the flap of the tent and shooed the little rat outside.

Dad picked up the nibbled apple core and tossed it to Marco. "What did Fiona say about leaving food in our tent?"

Marco had gone very quiet. He tossed the apple out of the tent and sat on his bed with his arms folded.

Mum gave Ria a hug. "Thank you, brave girl!" she said.

"You're my hero!" said Dad.

They all looked at Marco.

"Thanks, Ria," he mumbled, finally.

"That's okay," said Ria, as she climbed back into her sleeping bag and turned off the torch. She yawned. "Now, maybe I'll be able to get some sleep!"